Dad and Fifi

By Farley Frapples

Illustrated by Ruth Flannigan

Target Skill Consonant *Ff*/f/

Scott Foresman
is an imprint of

PEARSON

See Dad and Fif!

Fif can fit!

Dad can fan! Fan!

Can Fif fan?

Fan for Dad, Fif!

Fif can fan! Fan!

Look at Dad and Fif.
Dad and Fif fan!